Mense McInnis

Take The Jelly Off The Telly

Cover Illustrated by

Zhama Jumbo

Copyright© Mense McInnis 2023

All rights reserved

To everyone who encouraged me to share my writing with others.

Contents

Family 1
Senses 2
The Leaf.. 3
Exhausted 6
Healthy Eating 8
Come, Play With Me 10
Mutiny 12
The Snail.. 14
Night Life 16
The Submarine... 18
Take The Jelly Off The Telly 19
I Love Being Alone 21
No I Have Not 22
Knowing 23
Just Think 25
I Say What I Mean... 26
Voices From The Past 27
I Want To Be Saved By A Dragon 30
The Things We See Around Us 33
Going Nowhere Fast.. 34
If I Were An Animal.. 36
She's Gone... 37

The Ladder 39
The Grasshopper And The Ants 41
The Traffic Jam 43
Our Energy 44
Let's Play Pretend 45
Save The Best For Harold 47
The Seasons 48
   Summer flowers 48
   Autumn brings 49
   Winter blows 52
   Spring shouts. 54
Let's Talk 58
Unattainable 60
I Never Did 61
Have You Seen My Homework? 63
My Holiday 64
Maths Can Be Confusing 66

Family

She says she wants a dinosaur.
She says she wants a crane.
She wants to be a pilot.
Now she wants a plane.

She wants a Loch Ness monster.
Now she wants a train.
She wants to be an astronaut.
The moon will give her fame.

He has an old dinosaur.
He's got a broken crane.
He's got a book on pilots,
and a one winged aeroplane.

He tells her about the monster.
He's travelled miles by train.
He once met an astronaut.
Her moon landing gave her fame.

They sat and shared their ambitions.
They laughed, dreamed and sighed.
The difference…..
My dad's 91
My daughter's only 5.

Senses

Have you heard a dog whistle?
Seen a bull in a china shop.
Tasted a sour note
Touched wood for good luck.

Have you ever smelt a rat?
I wouldn't if I were you.
Some things are a mystery.
Some things are simply true.

Have you ever bent someone's ear
or kept yours to the ground.
Got up someone's nose.
Had a sniff around.

Have you seen a biscuit crumble
or a wound weep?
Kept honey so long, it finally fell asleep
or missed the bus by the skin of your teeth.

Have you seen a bear with a grudge
or a fish out of water?
Have you ever cut to the chase
or kissed a miner's daughter?

Have you got more luck than sense
or turned a blind eye?
I once heard through the grape vine;
if cat's got your tongue ...you can't lie.

The Leaf

At night I'm cold
Surrounded by fog
Shrouded in a watery veil.
Down below, people walk their dogs
While joggers run the jogging trail.

The morning mist begins to break
The sun glows on everyone.
Beyond the town.
Beyond the sea.
Boats sail on the horizon.

Families laze beneath our leaves,
Some picnic in our shade.
The younger ones play Hide and Seek.
Dogs on the river, bathe.

Children roll in the grass
Trip up over our roots
They all come to hug our bark,
Whispering their hidden truths.

Music plays under our leafy boughs,
Mouth watering smells, escape barbecues.
A flying lantern singes our leaves
Ice cream vans, lead mile long queues.

Migratory birds come flying through.
In their thousands.
In their swarms.
They follow the sun all year long
Just to keep their bodies warm.

When Autumn comes, their leaves fall off.
Their leaves just have to go.
The Mothers save all their energy
To survive the winter's snow.

I wish I was in the middle.
Where everyone can keep me warm.
The view up here is fantastic,
but the weather has lost its charm.

I hear the sound of a power saw.
Someone's cutting my Mother down.
Now he's dragging us through the forest,
placing us in the middle of the town.

From head to toe they've dressed us
in threads of rainbow silk.
Hanging balls of cotton clouds.
Tinsel of fairy ink.

The children camouflage Mother
with miles of wire and extra large bulbs.
Someone has just covered my eyes
with a shiny fairy glove.

Crowds begin to gather
Steam rises from their breath.
Music booms across the streets
Adding to the festiveness.

Everyone shouts. **5, 4, 3, 2, 1**
The Mayor flicks on the lights
We stand radiant in our beauty
A beacon in the darkness of the night starlight.

Children's mouths open in wonderment
The whole town stops to stare.
Glistening in our beauty
We shine. We dazzle. We dare.

From the eyes of everybody
Comes an outpouring of love
I feel the heat but cannot see anything
My eyes, still covered by that silly fairy glove.

Exhausted

Look at those feet?
Think of those toes?
Crushed into submission
by laces and bows.

Think of those feet,
squashed in those shoes.
Bunions in solitary
with no room to move.

Feet go in fast steps,
quick steps, short steps, long steps, Ssllooww.....
All moving in some direction
Some not knowing where to go.

Blacks and browns, constantly moving.
Tidal waves with glints of red.
Blues and greens are seldom seen,
treasured yellows even less.

I sit, watch and wonder,
puzzled by all those feet.
Where are they really rushing to?
Who are they going to meet?

Some belong to offices.
Some museums Some plays.
Some too late. Some too early
Yet they all rush, just the same.

Tsunami's of 8's and 11's,
Daily they pass by.
They never get any rest
Until lunchtime arrives.

It gives them a few precious minutes,
to take off their shoes and stretch.
They get the time to breathe for once,
before returning to their leather vests.

They eventually come to see me
This is what I do?
I work in a pedicure station.
I make feet beaut-i-ful.

Healthy Eating

Potatoes are not healthy
Neither broccoli nor rice.
I need something healthy
Please give me some advice?

I'm thinking about mint balls,
flying saucers or cherry lips.
How about black jacks and milk bottles
or even liquorice.

Carrots are not healthy
Neither cabbage nor green peas.
I want something healthy.
Can you help me please?

I'm thinking of some chewy sweets.
Boiled sweets, toffee sweets.
I'm thinking of something sugar free,
or something not too sweet.

They say sugar isn't good for you,
It'll take out all your teeth.
My dentist always shakes his head
whenever we should meet.

I think I'll have potatoes,
broccoli and rice.
Cabbage with green peas
I'll finally take his advice.

I want to have all my teeth
when I'm 64.
Not leave them in a glass at night,
like Henry's dad next door.

Come, Play With Me

Let's build castles and forests.
Dream of being brave.
Visit the sun for a nice cup of tea,
or the moon for a sleep in the shade.

Let's defeat the dragon in the wilderness.
Save the princess from the wicked witch.
Get the Lost Boys home for Christmas.
Throw the goblin into the ditch.

We can do this all on Monday, then
Tuesday it's the beach,
searching for buried treasure,
avoiding the pirates we might meet.

Snorkelling on the coral reefs,
under moonlit stars.
Let's go and find an octopus,
while swimming with the sharks.

Before you leave on Wednesday,
we'll go down to the park.
Climb mountains and chase dinosaurs.
Race horses in the dark.

A quick trip as astronauts.
Watching the universe grow.
We'll take a ride on a shooting star
Just before you go.

Next time you come to visit
We shall go on a safari.
Ride elephants, run with cheetahs
Or just ride in my Ferrari.

Mutiny

I'm standing in my bathroom.
On my window there's a fly.
On the ceiling fifty children
on their mother's web waving goodbye.

The rats are in the corner.
The mice behind the sink.
I wonder what is happening.
There is no time to think.

Nobody wants to live here.
They're leaving me alone.
They all want to move out,
to find a better home.

The cat's already in his cage.
The dog pulls him along.
The goldfish is complaining,
with a melancholy song.

The fleas hitchhike on dogs and cats
ready to depart.
Knowing that leaving,
will really break my heart.

They have found somewhere safer to live.
Somewhere, they'll never leave.
Somewhere more inviting.
Somewhere they all can breathe.

The snake preyed upon the cats.
The lizard on the fleas.
When they started disappearing,
they all decided to leave.

We were getting over crowded.
That is really true.
For all of them to leave at once
That they cannot do.

The Snail

He travelled upon a cushion of slime.
Behind him in his wake,
were spiders, caterpillars and ants.
Even the bones of a snake.

Deforestation followed behind him.
You had to predict where to go.
You've got to be quick to avoid him.
Even if he travels slow.

He slept like a submarine,
scanning from two long eyes.
His stalks were half an inch tall.
To him they reached the skies.

In his heart he was a glider,
travelling as fast as he can.
Everyone else saw devastation.
Nothing grew where he ran.

He wasn't really evil.
He was just born that way.
His eyes were taller than houses,
he could see that faraway.

He saw them drag Sally the lizard,
to their cemetery.
They bound and gagged and tied her up
in spider webbery.

Nobody crossed the spiders.
They always spread fear and dissent.
This time, however, they crossed the line,
now they had to repent.

He called out for his brothers.
They travelled on acid baths.
Straight into the nest of the spiders.
Making a treacherous path.

Sally was cocooned tightly.
Barely able to breathe.
They circled the place with destruction.
So she could safely leave.

Now, the snails are heroes.
Everyone wants them around.
They built them metal skateboards.
To safely guard the town.

Night Life

The moon's whiskers crept through my curtains.
Tickling my closed eyes.
I thought I was the only one.
Was I in for a surprise?

My lifeless toys reflected,
the glimmering night time light.
Sparkles mixed with fairy dust,
whiskers came from magic bright.

The jockey raced his horse.
The frogs began to croak.
Ken pushed Barbie in the pond,
and thought it was a joke.

The dolls line danced in the moonlight.
Dresses, shimmering free.
Action Man, chased two more Kens,
straight through the zebra's party.

Mother Hubbard was busy cooking.
Jack paid the old man for a cow.
The gingerbread's head was stuck in a jar.
The snake was taking a bow.

Below the ceiling, planes were flying.
World War VII in mid air.
Planets circling each other.
Stars glistening everywhere.

A family of balls, stopped at a level crossing.
A train passed by, chu- choo.
Jack could find no water.
Jill moved into the shoe.

Out from the dark walked the dinosaurs,
miniaturised by the T-Rex.
They sat in the moonlight reading a book,
about planets and Star Trek.

Monkey's trampolined across the bed,
with elephants and kangaroos.
Next were the flamingos,
all bought from London Zoo

The whiskers were getting shorter.
Muffled yawns, whispered, "Sleep tight."
Everyone went back to their places,
waiting for tomorrow night.

The Submarine

10,000, 15,000, 20,000, STOP.

 SILENCE.

NOBODY BREATHED. NOBODY MOVED.

LIGHTS FLICKERED AND CRACKLED,

FLASHES OF BLACK ON WHITE

ERRIE LIGHTNING AT MIDNIGHT.

FLASHES OF FACES, DISTORTED FACES

APPEARING, DISAPPEARING, REAPPEARING.

ENLARGED IN FLASHING LIGHT.

THE PANIC STRICKEN SUB

 LANDS ON THE SEABED

REVEBERATING LIKE AN EARTHQUAKE.

A MOMENT OF SILENCE

BEFORE THE PANIC STATRS.

SCREAMING, SHOUTING, CRYING

EVERYTHING NOT NAILED DOWN SLIDING

FROM LEFT TO RIGHT.

Take The Jelly Off The Telly

Take the jelly off the telly, the bowl is far too hot.
Take the jelly off the telly, it's going to collapse.
The Arctic's melting yellow, seagulls look confused.
The seals are bouncing off the ground,
deciding what to do.

Take the jelly off the telly, don't make me scream.
Take the jelly off the telly, why not put ice cream.
Down in the Antarctica, penguins like it ....not.
Now they're getting sunburnt,
their feet are getting hot.

Take the jelly off the telly, it needs to cool down first.
Take the jelly off the telly, a cloud's about to burst.
Farmers look up at the sky, it's raining red and green.
Animals are banning grass and eating jelly beans.

Take the jelly off the telly, it's sliding down the glass.
Take the jelly off the telly, it's settling inside fast.
The men are in the submarine, going out to sea.
Now the water's purple, while all the men are green.

Take the jelly off the telly, animals lick the screen.
Take the jelly off the telly, the crocodile's tongue
looks sherbert green.
There's a tongue from a snail, a tongue from a tiger.
A tongue from an antelope, but none from a spider.

Take the jelly off the telly, feet stuck in the grass.
Take the jelly off the telly, they cannot win or pass.

The goalie is waiting, a shot is coming through.
His knees have turned to jelly, His legs have gone to goo.

Take the jelly off the telly, the sun has gone all green.
Take the jelly off the telly, I'm about to scream.
The weatherman is sweating, he's drowning from the heat.
He's looking from his arm pits, to the puddles at his feet.

Take the jelly off the telly, Superman can't see.
Take the jelly off the telly, Spiderman's fallen from a tree.
Thor's hammer's not returning, Groot is getting wet.
Ant man's feeling funny, he's off to see the vet.

Take the jelly off the telly, the animals have gone blue.
Take the jelly off the telly, the fish are breathing goo.
The animals are wondering, what's happened to their tea?
It's usually grass and seeds, now it's straw-berry.

Take the jelly off the telly, lines travel across the screen.
Take the jelly of the telly, nothing can be seen.
I want to watch the weather. I want to see the news.
I'm watching a wobbly telly, about to blow a fuse.

I Love Being Alone

I want to be a tortoise.
I want to be a stone.
I want to be a midnight star
I want to be left alone.

I want to be a glow worm
and glow and glow and glow.
If I should ever fade away,
I want no one to know.

Can you keep a secret?
I like my solitude.
The world today's too noisy.
The people are so rude.

I want to be an oyster,
keep my precious stone.
Just be precious to myself
and be left alone.

I want to be a shooting star,
travelling across the sky.
Looking down upon the world
waving you all goodbye.

No I Have Not

Have you seen a lipity lap on a lippity lap loot

or a tippity tap on a hippity hap with a hippity hap hoot.

Out there walks a sippity snap with three snippity snap snoots

Looking for peace from the trippity trap, glippity glap gloots.

Knowing

I know
you know, that you know,
what you do not know.

If you do know, that you do not know,
what you want to know, you should know
just where to go.

Ask someone who should know
Ask your parents?
Ask a teacher?
Ask a friend?

We all have a craving, a curiosity.
Why do you think babies smile
when they realise
we understand them
when they speak

Societies have been built upon
what we already know.
Discoveries and inventions tested
for what we really don't.

 Science, Maths and DT.
Are very useful I would say
to answer this question.
Why do tree trunks only come in grey?

That is why we are so far,
from the days of the dinosaur.

When we know,
that we do not know,
what we want to.
We go out and explore.

We have to know
what we do not know
to let everyone know
now we know exactly what to do.

Just Think

Grass here is forever blue.
Sky is always green.
Mountains glisten rainbows.
The quiet is serene.

Women robe in clouds of white,
Men in Pluto's rings,
I just like the simple life,
The simple life of kings.

Girls dazzle like Athena,
Boys overdress like Zeus,
Everyone travels by crocodile
or snail with a turbo boost.

 If you can't take the speed
there's another option;
Travel by snake with flamingo wings
Or borrow grandpa's oxen.

I Say What I Mean

No silver lining in my cloud.
My cloud is lined with lead.
Always under the weather.
Pets falling on my head.

The ball has never been in my court.
It falls outside the crease.
My glass is always half empty
I survive by the skin of my teeth.

I hate to beat around the bush.
I'm really as right as rain.
My life's as sweet as angel's wings.
I refuse to go down in flames.

Voices From The Past

It is the midnight hour.
Mist emanates from the ground.
The night is still and soundless.
Sighing mist is all around.

Slow white misty tendrils
get shinier as dawn breaks.
Gently, lights begin to blink
as villagers awake.

In-between the night and dark
birds begin to twitter.
The early birds get the juiciest worms.
The late ones have no dinner.

Early workers leave their homes
in clouds of swirling mist.
A pause follows school children
greeting a fiery fist.

The mist begins to dissipate
when out comes all the mums
Filling local shopping malls.
Pulling toddlers, pushing prams.

The fist of fire rises
in the middle of a transparent sky.
A foghorn echoes silence.
Everyone stops to sigh.

Everybody heads east.
Some begin to cry.
Everybody heads to where
soldiers go when they die.

The spot is marked by a stone.
Steps lead underground.
They make an orderly caterpillar.
As they snake underground.

It's light, dry and airy,
bulbs twinkle, coral in the sea.
In the centre are tables and benches.
In the middle of those an oak tree.

The walls are copper plated
with shiny letterbox slots.
Around them, ceremonial images
tied with forget-me-nots.

You can hear a baby whimper.
The rocking of a pram.
The rhythmic breathing of body heat.
The snoring from a gran.

Where they stand is cavernous.
The size of a large village.
The walls are covered with letterbox slots.
The higher the slot the more privilege.

A foghorn echoed deep inside,
and out from the creaking walls,

came toes, fingers, ears and eyes
with a half blown up football.

The walls gave birth in its hundreds.
The living mixed with the dead.
They all caught up on the latest news.
A year's worth, in hours was said.

Children met great, great, grandparents.
Uncles, aunts, cousins and grans.
Stories of folk lore and escapades,
smiles and laughter did span.

A foghorn wailed a little longer.
The dead sadly went back to their graves.
Shared memories made the community stronger.
On the walls were the beds of the brave.

 Everyone filed out.
With bitter sweet memories.
Next year, same day, same time.
They will reunite more families.

I Want To Be Saved By A Dragon

A dragon emerged from the slime.
To fly a thousand miles.
The day he left his family,
his son was filled with smiles.

The prince woke up had breakfast,
covered in jam tarts.
He wanted to be a dragon slayer.
Today he'll make a start.
There were none in his area,
so that broke his heart.

In his castle he locked up the princess.
From her eye fell a single tear.
She longed to fly through fluffy clouds,
while wind passed through her hair.
She wanted to be saved by a dragon.
Green or blue she did not care.

The dragon spotted the castle,
from a hundred miles away.
He turned to fly from East to West.
She took his breath away.
There he saw the most delicate thing
his family could eat in a day.

With scales, claws and green-blue skin,
he hopes she doesn't stare.
He thinks she might need rescuing
but he does not care.

He wouldn't want to scare her.
Just take her to his lair.

The prince he saw a glint of green,
then blue, a flash of light.
"That I'm sure is a dragon,
this is now my fight."
With sword and steel and armour,
he rode towards daylight.

He couldn't climb the castle steps.
He called the princess down.
He shouted, "Here comes a dragon!"
and chained her to the ground.
The princess screamed, pretended to faint,
then winked and hit the ground.

With fiery breath, he swooped,
just as the prince raised his sword.
The princess peered out of one eye,
pretending to be distraught.
"Come dragon, come and save me.
Take me to your court."

The sky suddenly got murky.
The clouds, a greyish white.
The rain began to drizzle
and the enemies stopped the fight.
They ran into the kitchen to wait another night.

The princess wanted to be a queen.
The prince to be a king.

The dragon was tired of running
His part was so boring
He saw a squirrel run up a tree
and wanted to bark at him.

How could the performance be better?
In the morning they'll make a start.
For now they'll drink their warm milk
and eat some more jam tarts.

The Things We See Around Us

The things we see around us
are wondrous indeed.
Sometimes they go by slowly
Sometimes they go with speed

From the colours of the rainbow.
The blues, the gold's, the greens.
There are Autumn leaves, from rustic brown
to red and aubergine.

Wonders are all around us,
the snails, the worms, the slugs.
Centipedes and millipedes,
six legged ants and four legged bugs.

There's the eight legged spider.
The two legged kangaroo.
I hear you shout impossible.
Watch closely at the zoo.

The wonders of the universe.
From sky to earth to sea,
are all worth exploring,
by better minds than me.

Going Nowhere Fast

Stuck in a traffic jam
hurriedly going nowhere.
Mr Snail glides by with his family
all I do is stare.

Through the rear view mirror,
I see the snaking traffic.
Carleen's banana slug
could make a yummy sandwich.

Bored children cry and argue.
Apple cores thrown through windows.
Bikes weave through the traffic.
Parents thinking, 'We must buy one of those.'

On windscreens bugs are racing.
Clouds morphing, as grass grows.
Noisy boredom is so loud.
Listen to the horns echo.

Tyres move in honey.
The air pollution's bad.
By the time we finally get out of here,
I'll be as old as my great granddad.

I can feel the hair on my head growing.
My nails are hooked like claws.
We've moved four feet in one go.
Listen to the wave of applause.

The apple seeds, thrown out this morning,
have now started to grow.
When I left home it was summer,
now it's starting to snow

If I Were An Animal

I want to be an elephant,
reaching branches only giraffes can,
splashing water, spraying flowers
before the hose pipe ban.

I want to be a panther,
sleek, shiny and slim,
walking silently through the jungle,
wearing a coat that's shimmering.

I want to be a turtle,
nowhere to go, nobody to see.
never rushing for anything,
enjoying nature surrounding me.

I want to be a snake,
slithering, sliding, gliding as i go
hissing, always searching for someone
for a rat a mouse or baby crow.

I want to be a cat.
a black cat with white spots over my eyes,
fourteen hour days lazing on the radiator,
looking at the skies.

i want to be a porcupine
nobody could brush my hair
all who approach me
handle with care.

She's Gone
She disappeared in a puff of smoke.
She brought me to school then went to work.
I had a lot to say. She barely spoke.
She was busy washing, ironing, getting dinner ready.
I watched TV, did my homework and ate all my spaghetti.

She disappeared in a puff of smoke.
I walked to school. She drove to work.
I had a lot to say. She guided my thoughts when I spoke.
I was busy reading, studying, exploring.
Staying out late, exams in the morning.
She always chuckled at my jokes.

She disappeared in a puff of smoke.
I was a pioneer, charting my course.
I came back often; I had a lot to say.
She listened when I spoke.
She heard them all before
but still laughed at my jokes.

She disappeared in a puff of smoke.
I had started to grey.
She was locked inside.
Tendrils of recognition in her eyes.
She smiled when I spoke of times gone by.
There was no reply.
A tear in her eye, said she spoke.

She disappeared in a puff of smoke.
She lay silently, eyes closed.
Dressed in pink and flowered bows.
STILL.
We held hands and buried her on a hill of smoke.

The Ladder

I looked into his eyes.
He looked right back at me.
He is my son's son.
He will grow to know me.
He is family.

I will tell him about the ladder.
Tell him about the wall.
Tell him that, "The higher you climb
the harder you will fall."

When you build your ladder.
You might lose some nails.
Cut some rungs a bit too short.
Or even want to bail.

They won't tell him about the ladder.
They will about the wall.
He might have to work twice as hard,
to get a softer fall.

There will always be others,
scaling walls with relative ease.
Lying at the foot will be thousands
who thought they were born to succeed.

Many will discourage you.
"Talented for running, rapping, and
getting in debt.
No talent, no ambition.
No focus, no depth."

You are allowed to scale the wall.
For the most of us five bricks up.
Enough to feed your family,
take a holiday and shut up.

For some the sky's the limit.
For others the limit's the sky.
He's going to need the ladder,
I'm leaving for him to climb.

Everybody needs a ladder.
Once built it lasts for life.
Your great, great, great, grand children,
will thank you for easing their strife.

Some never build a ladder.
Some pull it up from behind.
Some build one every day.
Some are hard to find.

Don't worry about the height of the wall.
Build a ladder you can climb.
If yours is little too short,
just put it on top of mine.

The Grasshopper And The Ants

I constantly tell the tale
of the grasshopper and the ants.
The hopper he loved to have fun
While the ants were moving plants.

Hopper played, danced and partied.
His mantra was You Only Live Once.
The ants they had backbreaking work,
carrying leaves for months and months

The hopper stopped the procession.
He would play, hoping they would dance.
They paused, shook their heads and kept working,
looking at him askance.

"How silly can you be," he shouted,
"the breeze is cool, the weather is fine.
Don't worry about tomorrow,
you have the wrong things on your mind."

He danced until his hat fell off.
He danced holes into his shoes.
He played that fiddle until its strings broke,
then laughed at the ants. How rude.

Autumn followed Summer.
Followed by Winter's snow.

Nothing left but the clothes on his back,
he had to burn his bow.

Little white spots beat down mercilessly.
Snow frozen to his bones.
Trailing footprints two feet deep.
He had nowhere to go.

He wasted time with the violin.
He wasted time with the dance.
He lived a reckless, careless life.
He lived a life of chance.

The ants were dancing merrily,
when a half dead grasshopper fell by.
They warmed him up and fed him
Frozen tears fell from his eyes.

Always use your time wisely
Think sensibly
Always plan for your future
Don't be like me.

The Traffic Jam

I'm in a traffic jam, I can't get out. I'm in
a traffic
jam, someone help me out. Open the
door, move your car, pull me through the
roof from a far.
Just get me out of this jam jar?
I'm in a traffic jam I can't get out.

I'm in lockdown with 70 million others.
I'm in lockdown, the TV is my mother.
I'm stuck watching TV,
listening the news, hearing the voices of
everyone else has left me so confused.
I'm in lock down can't see no way out.
I'm stuck indoors, they won't let me out.

I'm afraid of going outside.
Afraid of opening my front door.
I'm afraid of the outside,
I can't take it anymore.
My teeth are falling out,
my hair is getting thin
I've been left alone so long the walls are
closing in.
I've got claustrophobia, agoraphobia,
pulling from within.
I'm afraid of the outside and the outside
is not coming in.

Our Energy

There's a light I cannot see.
There's a light I hear surrounding me.
Should I let it come
Should I let it go
Indecisiveness
I do not know.
Is it in my mind
Is it in my heart
Wherever it is
my head's being pulled apart.
There's a light I hear surrounding me
There's a light
I cannot see.

Let's Play Pretend

I will be a dragon, breathing fire through my mouth.
You can be an octopus in warm waters heading South.
I will fly to find you, wherever you might be.
If you want to play pretend, just phone me.

I will be a caterpillar, in a warm cocoon.
You can be an astronaut and fly me to the moon.
I will crawl to find you, wherever you might be.
If you need to play pretend, just phone me.

I will be an acrobat, juggling balls and chairs.
You can be a hamster running circles everywhere.
I will jump to find you, wherever you might be.
If you need to play pretend, just phone me.

I will be a butterfly, wearing green and gold.
You can be a light house with sea stories untold.

I will flutter to find, you wherever you might be.
If you need to play pretend, just phone me.

I will be a strong knight, fighting dragons with sharp teeth.
You can be the horse, my friend, my trusted steed.
I will be brave to find you wherever you might be.
If you need to play pretend just phone me.

Save The Best For Harold

I'll have cabbage and save the corn beef for Harold.
I'll have fish and save the chips for Harold.
I'll have avocado and save the toast for Harold.
I'll have cauliflower and save the curry for Harold.

I'll have asparagus and save the salmon for Harold.
I'll have sprouts and save the beef for Harold.
I'll have soup and save the ice cream for Harold
I'll have water and save the trifle for Harold.

Harold isn't coming
He cannot behave
He just phoned this morning.
Not to bring all the things I saved
He says his Mum might let him out later in the week
As I'm his best friend I get them all to eat.

The Seasons

Summer flowers stared at the summer's sun
half shading their eyes with their petals.
A light wind laughed as dandelion seeds,
with white dreadlocks, got tangled in the nettles.
Some clipped the heads of buttercups
Without even saying pardon.
On days like this sharp elbows are used to
start a new life in next door's garden.

It was always like this during summer.

Avoiding lupine, lavender and magnolia.
Those who made it were in for a surprise.
Next door's recent delivery, was a shock to everyone's eyes.
On the decking, hummed an electric lawn mower, whose smile was as wide as their cries.
Some screamed for the wind to blow slower'
Some screamed for rain, to come down from the skies.

It was always like this during summer.

Snap dragons argue with fox gloves.
While sweet peas, cover their children's

ears. Trying to block out the shouting,
from rude flowers living so near.
The bees come out collecting,
pollen in their little jugs.
They will not collect from any flowers
Who show each other no love.

It was always like this during summer.

Hopping from flower to flower
are yellow heads, wings and feet.
Dusted with yellow icing sugar,
which is going to taste so sweet

Ants keep on working.
They have a lot to clear.
Sugared ants sneezing from hay fever.
During the summer months of the year.
It never stops them feeding the colony
Garden life's going through its usual routine.
storing up for the approaching winter.
There has to be enough food to feed The Queen

Autumn brings
Shadowing, stalking, hunting.
Like a preying bird she waits.
She oozes like liquid jelly through the town
Simultaneously from above

and below the ground.
Submerging everyone and everything
While the clouds break down
sieved through frozen fingers,
on roof tops, parks and towns.

She blankets us with her shroud
A white silk duvet bubble above houses and trees
Insulated, protected, in her freeze,
She bites.
With nibbling baby teeth, she bites,
A little sharper, a little deeper,
relaying a warning.
Suit-cased swallows and swifts,
cookie cut, descending mists
For warmer climates
To rejoice with their siblings and chicks

Worms, snails, slugs,
hibernate with sleeping bugs
Who bury themselves, deep below,
where they hope the frost can't reach.
Tree hearts slow until their falling hair
Rests gently at their feet
Providing warmth to the hibernated
Who snuggle a little deeper below the thickening sheet.
She bites.

Some made of paper, some of wood
Streams throw boats onto the shore
Sunken boats, shipwrecked like bones
Waiting, rooted to sail away once more.
There lay the boats of fore parents from a long time ago.
Aeroplanes which never made it across
Point tail fins at the sky
Lakes give off a mirrored glow
Reflections fractured by the concentric waves
of children throwing stones.

Peacock preening trees, strut their fashion show.
Bringing all the styles which took a year to grow.
In their glory they shine.
Children stop and stare at a beautiful sight
Brown, red, purple and yellow hues of absolute delight
Puff jacketed people move faster, as shorter days bring longer nights
Lights stay on longer
Darkness surrounds us as she bites

People can hardly see, where they want to go.
Trucks bring wood to nearby parks,

to warm frozen, hearts tomorrow.
Fires make crackling sounds warming thousands in one go.
The wind bites in earnest, everyone has a frozen nose.
Visitors look skyward not knowing what to see
Rockets burst overhead followed by shouts of glee.
That's what it's like in the park
For three hours on Bonfire Night.

Winter blows in and arrives with frozen dandruff.
He thanks his sister for paving the way.
They have done this every year, a million times
before today.
Bald trees stare down on tracing paper.
Footprints make dot to dot.
Cars belch smoke like frightened squids.
Smiling children at class windows
are getting hot.

The heating stays on longer
Children watch TV in bed
People indoors are happy to be alive
Statues, glad to be dead.
Temperatures drop to minus

Some say it's minus 23
No matter the time of day or night
the roads are constanhtly busy.
Among the lights appear reds and greens
with lots and lots of gold.
Angel wings are all around
with gifts the Three Kings hold.
Everybody sings at least one song
about people more than 2,000 years old

Nonstop laughter and celebrations.
Queues stretch like the tide,
gathering food and presents,
families fly in from miles.
Santa's very busy
he's dressed in black, green and gold
He's complaining that his red and white
makes him look too old.

With bellies full, there's snoring.
Presents abandoned on the floor.
The cat kisses the dog under the mistletoe,
once a year and no more.
The whole country's heaving.
The New Year comes in with Big Ben.
A blaze of sparks, bangs and shouting.
Hands join for the song at the end

Resolutions last for hours,
A few might last for days.

Exercise and diets,
Some start and end on New Year's Day.
Everyone's quiet
Everyone's sad
Too much of what they had was spent
to give those who did not have.
"The children will never forget,"
someone shouts,
While another shouts, "Be quiet!
I have a head the size of a whale's
tongue.
and I have to be at work tonight."

The snow comes down in blizzards.
For days no one has seen the sun.
A happy New Year to everyone
this weather will not last long.

Spring shouts.
With a frown turned upside down.
Ice melts.
Birds in their millions come back home.
Parks slowly fill as children play.
Asking, "Was the sun away on holiday?"

Streams and rivers flow again,
fish are caught and let go.
The heart of the park begins to beat
from the tops of trees, hair grows.

The year has come full circle.
Migratory birds come home to roost.
They look forward to warmer weather
The sun's finally unloosed

The seasonal move is bitter sweet.
Sunburnt from their break,
They take up residence in the trees,
to sit and patiently wait.
The undergrowth has awoken,
those birds are very smart.
They feed on butterflies, moths, beetles
and bugs, while pulling the leaves apart.

Silk scarves replaced by sandy mist
From underneath the trees
Flies, frogs, slugs and wasps
Stretch from a duvet of leaves
Hoping to squat 'till summer
knowing when Autumn comes,
they will have to leave.

Missing You
I miss her touch.
I miss her smell.
I missed her

when she jumped
off the stairs and fell
onto the radiator.

The ambulance came,
blue lights blaring.
Through frosted windows,
the whole street staring.
Behind twitching curtains
Waiting for someone to be taken to A&E
It was a sprain not a break luckily.

I missed her when she went to school
An oversized rucksack carried her tools
All those term breaks throughout the years
I miss them with her I do declare
We had the best fun throughout those early years
How I really miss her

At secondary school.
Her fashion became a different style
Lipstick, eyeliner, t-shirt logos undefined
With slogans from which I would run a mile

Now she walks in unrecognised,
In boots I never knew existed.

She passed away one day, last year.
From my eye not a single tear
Her voice rings loudly in my ear
"Hey Dad, I'm still over here."
Yes, she knows I miss her.

Let's Talk

Come let's talk just us two.
Tell me what is worrying you.
All those things you wanted to see.
All those dreams you wanted to achieve.
Those nightmares which will not allow you to breath
Come and talk to me.

Tell me those things which make you cry.
The things which make you feel quite shy.
The hurdles you overcame
Which made you cry
Those things which kept you safe inside
Come and talk to me

Lay on your back and deeply breathe.
Look at the sun glinting through the trees.
Feel the energy it gives us.
Leaves block the sun
But opportunities come through for everyone
Come and talk to me

Stand upon the river bank.
Watch stones skip out of reach.
Concentric circles touch the shore like memories
Then sink into the deep.
The other bank, they will try to stride, but

will never reach.
Come and talk to me.

Tell me your pains, your woes and your sorrows
Give me your burden to share.
Be focused on what you want to achieve
You will be going to uni next year.
Come and talk to me.

Unattainable

They are not a million miles away
They are in my head
Because I cannot get them out
I cannot go to bed

My family is so far away
I can't make it in one step
It's going to take a lot of work
And a very, very fast jet.

Scary stories give me goose bumps.
I grab them but they're gone
A thousand come up on my arm, and yet,
I have never caught even one.

There are a thousand sweets in the glass jar
above the kitchen sink.
It's too high for me to reach it
But low enough for my finger tip.

Of the things I could do
with one thousand chews
and those brains
which taste sugary sweet

Nothing is really out of reach
You can be who you want to become
You just have to put in the ground work
Remembering your priorities are number one.

I Never Did
Fit in
at school
I sat
in a corner
and
wept.
It rained on me every day
Until the white clouds in my blue sky bled.

> MR Motivator came in to school one day
> And left us some sound advice
> "You do not have to be stuck in a rut
> to get the best out of life."
>
> "I was on a hamster's wheel
> Going nowhere fast
> Someone gave me permission
> to change my life at last."
>
> "Today I say to you boys and girls
> who listen to my voice
> Go ahead and change right now
> Make that positive choice."
>
> I listened to what he had to say
> and what he said was true.
> From that day I decided,
> to change my attitude.
> All I had to remember,
> Schools throw opportunities at you?

But instead of picking them up
I stepped on them with my feet.
The more I listened, the more I learnt
My confidence stepped upon my defeat.

Those rainy clouds were summer bright
In Winter and in storms.
All through the days,
all through the nights
My dark days are Summer warm.

Be who you want to be,
You have dreams you want to achieve.
Be patient.
Start collecting opportunities,
you will be surprised where they can lead.

Have You Seen My Homework?

Have you seen my shoes?
Have you seen where I put my pen?
I have to get to school?

Who has moved my keys?
Who has got my comb?
Polly needs to be in her cage?
She can't be left alone?

Someone's taken my mobile phone?
Where's my iron shirt?
Where's all the work I did last night?
Where is this morning's work?

The food in the fridge has gone missing?
The cupboard is empty too?
Animals are in the back garden?
What are they going to do?

There's the cat, the dog, and Polly,
serving all the pets in the neighbourhood.
Plus crickets and wasps, bees and bugs
Snails and slugs and anything that
squirms.

They have a Las Vegas sign in the garden:
"Please remember to thank
the people of this lovely house
for contributing to this food bank."

Maths Can Be Confusing

The first day I came to school
I could already add
I knew how to take away
But!!!
The things they want me now to do
Make me really mad.

Our teacher asks for:
more of, groups of, you need to increase,
how many more can you add on?
how much more does he need?

Then she asks us:
to find the sum, you have to plus and repeat
get them altogether, get the total,
he is going to need more feet

Then she taught us to subtract
which started really fine.
Find what remains, how many are left behind.
Take out those who are unhappy
Keep those who are being kind.

Minus, reduce, subtract and take away.
What more is left to find?
I scream, when she talks about,
there is more or less to find.

My teacher's going crazy
She can't make up her mind.

He is not content for us to multiply,
Are you not confused?
When you have to double, triple
or convert a square number
to its square root.

One minute she wants us to multiply,
next she wants to increase.
Why does she not say what she wants
and leave us all in peace

I really want to give up.
She wrote 1 to 39
Now she says prime numbers
are really easy to find.

She's putting dots in triangles
She'll soon be putting dots in squares
If she wants to play dot to dot
I'd rather play musical chairs.

She came in this morning
with her arm in a sling.
We all were sorry for her
but it was just the start of things.

She said, "This is the starter of our maths lesson. My arm has been broken at an angle."

And then she started to draw
A straight line, acute, obtuse and reflex
angle

I wondered if she had broken both of
them,
Would she have stayed at home ?
or would she still come into class
and double our work load?